# THE NEW GUY

# THE NEW GUY

## JASON PEACOCK

The New Guy

**BOOKLOGIX®**
Alpharetta, Georgia

ISBN: 978-1-61005-075-3

Printed in the United States of America

∞This paper meets the requirements of ANSI/NISO Z39.48-1992 (Permanence of Paper)

# Table of Contents

# Foreword

It was our Master's Sunday; we had just won our flight & successfully battled through the elimination round at Jason's member guest tournament. We found ourselves sitting on the back tee box of Achasta's long, heart-retching 18th hole featuring a narrow fairway lined with water, eagerly waiting to catch a leaky drive, or chunked fairway shot to the green. Hooting and hollering fans were packed in down the fairway standing way too close for the skill set of these two weekend hackers. Then the unimaginable happened. The scratch golfers, not to mention current club champions we were competing against (both equipped with Ernie Els swings and Tiger Woods mental focus), gave in under the pressure and shanked their tee shots giving us the clear advantage to victory. This was the defining moment of the match, our golf careers, and my friendship with Jason. As I placed my driver back into my bag and reached for my 5-wood, Jason, shook his head saying, "That's not what brought us to this dance; put that away...WE are hitting the BIG STICKS!"

In sales, as in life, you sometimes need to lay it all on the line leaving every ounce of effort on the course. For The New Guy, this book is your golden ticket on how you can stand up on that first tee and differentiate yourself from all of your would-be competitors. Jason will not only coach you to become much better positioned for selling, but his tips will also help you create a rewarding career filled with lifelong customers, friendships, and double-eagle deals. I wish I had been equipped with this book in my bag when I started out my career.

For those of us seasoned sales veterans who have spent most of our careers trading in putters, teeing up Pro V1s and chasing 300 yard drives into the woods (finding Top Flites); this book is also for you. You will enjoy reminiscing about many of the same sales adventures (and mis-adventures) Jason faced early in his round as a NEW GUY. This book will also help you de-clutter your pre-shot routine allowing for laser focus of your time on those back-nine activities we already know bring us the best results: SELLING.

Jeffrey S. Dunn, CIC

Senior Casualty Broker

CRC Insurance

# Acknowledgements

To my wife Wendy: There is an ancient proverb that asks the question: "A wife of noble character...who can find?" Thankfully, I did. There are not enough pages to contain my thankfulness for you. My life's dream came true when you said yes.

To my kids: Tanner, Cameron, and Kylee. You are my pride and joy.

To my Mom & Dad: You have always been in my corner, and for that I am eternally grateful.

To my brothers Justin & Jon: You are more than brothers...you are my best friends.

To my Granny Katherine: You have shown me by example that "Attitude is everything."

To Tricia Hushmire: You are a great teammate and thank you for making me look a lot better than I am.

To Bruce Eades: Thank you for being my mentor and big brother.

To the team at IOA: We have way too much fun to be in the insurance business!

And finally to you, the New Guy: You are the reason I wrote this.

# Introduction

The New Guy. You know him. You might be him, or at the very least, you were him. Remember being "The New Guy?" If you just started in the business, think back to last week or earlier this morning. Being the new guy is a rite of passage. When the office is decorating the Christmas tree, guess who gets the honor of pulling the tree out of storage? Yep, the New Guy. When anything heavy needs to be lifted including, but not limited to, copy machines, trash cans, dead files, file cabinets, or typewriters from the 1950s, guess who gets the hernia? That's right...same guy. Being the New Guy brings with it a few minor benefits. For starters, you are not expected to pick up the tab at lunch because everybody knows you're broke and you get to hear about all the ailments that afflict your coworkers and actually act interested. If any of the above sounds familiar, this book is for you.

Before we go any further, let me at least tell you who I am so you will know who to send fan mail to. My name is Jason Peacock, and for the last twenty-one years I have been engaged in the world of sales. I eased my way into the business at age eighteen by selling newspaper subscriptions door-to-door in Chicago. I continued to climb the corporate ladder by parlaying that job into a stint as a telemarketer selling five year subscriptions for various magazines. Yes, you read right...five years! Along the way, I sold everything from college alumni directories, carpet cleaning services, hand warming devices, air purification systems, and even had a brief career in retail at a clothing store, which makes perfect sense for someone who is completely color blind! For over a decade now, I have had the pleasure of selling insurance as an independent agent. I am not a Rhodes Scholar, although I did spend a lot of time on the road...between the several colleges I attended.

I am just like you. I have a family: One incredible wife, three amazing kids, and two proud parents. I live in a middle class neighborhood, drive a used car, and my hobbies include losing golf balls and gaining weight! Don't you feel better about yourself already? OK, now you are really wondering why you bought this book. Hang on, it gets better. This book is about the rainy Mondays, sunny Fridays, and the mundane Wednesdays that make us want to throw on the blue vest and greet at Wal-Mart. You know what I'm talking about, don't you? If you have been in the sales game for any length of time you have experienced some of each of those days, quite possibly in the same week!

The inspiration behind this book came to me as I returned home from a meeting in Charlotte, North Carolina. The date was October 31, 2006. I should have known that scheduling an appointment on Halloween wasn't a good idea. Believe me, this meeting turned into all trick and no treat! The meeting started out as they all do...small talk, the passing of business cards, the usual banter about the weather, etc. When it came time for me to make my presentation, something happened to me that had never happened before. I panicked. If you have never had a panic attack, let me try to put it in perspective for you: Think of a time when you were scared, embarrassed, clueless, speechless, and throw in a good dose of amnesia and there you have it...a panic attack. I excused myself from the meeting and went to the bathroom, hoping to find some composure. What I found instead was a sweaty wreck staring back at me in the mirror. I eventually made my way back into the board room, apologized for the disaster that had just transpired, and left. Thank the Lord there isn't a cliff to drive off of between Charlotte and Atlanta or you probably wouldn't be reading this. Somewhere along Interstate 85, a thought came to me: Selling is Hard! It's not easy putting yourself "out there" everyday. Rejection, fear, pressure and disappointment are something we in the sales profession face every day. On that ride home, I made a commitment to myself. I would do everything I could to help other sales professionals win. Win sales, win at relationships, win personal victories, and win in life. That's how this book came into being. What began as a failure would become a victory.

Alright, enough about me, let's talk about you. Why are you in sales? C'mon now...don't tell me that you went to the wrong booth at Career Day! Seriously, why does anyone sell? I am writing this on a laptop computer—a computer that has more technology in it than NASA had when they put a man on the moon. In the Digital Age, why does anyone need us? While the products we sell come and go, our profession is still alive and kicking. The earliest use of the word "salesman" goes all the way back to the year 1523; just a few years after the original "Sails-man" Christopher Columbus sailed the Ocean Blue. Think about that. Salespeople have been around forever... from "Capt. Chris" navigating the Atlantic to Taurus-driving Tom navigating rush hour, the brethren of selling has stood the test of time.

Now back to my question: why did you go into sales? Perhaps you were told that you were a "born salesman," or that you have the gift of gab so surely sales is the place for you. Maybe you majored in Business Administration, and upon graduation you quickly learned that companies don't hire twenty-two-year-olds to "Administer" business. Given the current economy, you may have been down-sized from middle or upper management, and now the only meeting you are concerned about is meeting quota. Whatever brought you here is irrelevant. Just like the arrow says on the map at the mall: You are here.

If you have used MapQuest, you know that to find out how to get to where you want to go, you need to know where you are starting from. You are starting from the very place that every business that has ever existed starts from...Sales. At one point in time, someone sold the first pair of Nikes (and by the way, my Dad is convinced that he bought them...and yes, he still wears them). Sales is a noble profession. Consider this: we are the only ones in a company that produce the Top Line. I have noticed one thing about our recent economic challenge—there isn't a single company in the world who is trying to sell less. Sales is the ultimate job security. If you can bring business in the door, you will never be without a job. Top salespeople have always been, and always will be, in demand.

When you finish reading this book, I want you to come away from the experience with a new perspective on what you and I do for a living. One of my favorite quotes is from a French guy whose name I can't pronounce. He says:

In everything there is an unexplored element, because we are prone to use our eyes only in combination with the memory of what others before us have thought of the same thing we are looking at. The most insignificant thing contains some little unknown element. We must find it!

*-Maupassant.*

Now, go get your business card. What does your title say? I'll bet the word "sales" is nowhere on it, is it? Sounds like we have some work to do.

-Jason Peacock

# Chapter 1

# Getting Out
# of the Blocks

*"Good things come to those who wait...but only the things left behind by those who hustle."*

- Abraham Lincoln

I will never forget the time I challenged my dad to a race. I was about eleven years old and due to my stellar record of racing triumphs at recess, I was positive that I could take down my Pops. He was a former high school football star with exploits much like Al Bundy, and I figured if I could beat him, there wasn't a kid alive who could touch me. When we lined up in our yard, my dad did something I had never seen: He got down in a sprinters stance while I remained in an upright position. My mom, who stood at the finish line some fifty yards away, was the starter. "On your mark...get set...go!" What happened next is all a blur. Not because of speed, but because I was on the receiving end of a vicious elbow to the bread basket. With elbows pumping, knees churning, and breathing like a freight train, my dad "took me to school"...old school that is. Unbeknownst to me, the correct way to come out of the starting blocks is with a flurry of activity. The elbow? Simply a casualty on the field of battle. Nothing personal, I just happened to be in the way.

The game of selling is very similar to a race. Although it's not a sprint, the importance of getting out of the blocks is vital. Remember when you started? If you are brand new, just think about last week. See if this rings a bell: You show up at your new office/cubicle/phone booth/whatever workspace you were given at quarter 'til eight on Monday morning. You walk in briskly, whistling of course, say hello to the receptionist, sit down, and by 7:50 a.m., you are wondering: "What do I do now?!" Of course the veterans are in the break room eating donuts, drinking coffee, and catching up on the past weekends' games. So you figure, "Hey, I'm one of the guys. I will just hang out for a while and shoot the bull." After a half hour of bull-shooting, you return to your workspace hoping for an email, voice mail, smoke signal, or Morse code...anything that would indicate that someone wants to talk with you, or better yet, wants to buy from you. Wait...the phone's ringing...you answer it in the most professional voice you can muster, "John Smith." Oh, it's just the HR department needing more paperwork signed.

AT APPROXIMATELY 10 A.M., A THOUGHT HITS YOU: "WHAT IF THE PHONE NEVER RINGS?" THE NEXT THING I AM GOING TO SAY WILL CHANGE YOUR SELLING LIFE IF YOU LET IT... *THE PHONE WILL NOT RING!!!*

The Graveyard of Sales is full of tombstones that read, "The phone never rang." If you came into this business expecting business to immediately fall into your lap, let me do you a favor: That HR person that just called? Have them go ahead and draw up your separation notice and conduct your exit interview, because you ain't gonna make it. No matter how well you scored on your personality profile or whether or not you graduated Summa Cum Laude, Magna Cum Laude, or "By the Grace of Lordy," if you are waiting for folks to come to you, you best head to Kinko's and get some more resumes printed. You may be sitting there saying, "Jason, that may be the case for most rookies, but what you don't know is that one of my fraternity brothers is a vice president at a local bank."

Well Sparky, the good news is that he is a vice president; the bad news is that his business cards were printed in pencil! While your relationship with Mr. Banker may pay dividends down the road, it may not help you a whole bunch right now seeing as though the ink is still drying on your stationary. By the time you get done with your training, odds are that Mr. Banker will no longer be with the bank he was with a month ago.

If you are a seasoned sales professional or sales manager, what I am about to say will probably cause you to bristle. Ready? Most companies instruct their new salesmen and saleswomen to make a list of everyone they know and immediately start calling on them. My question is: Why? I know, I know, I might as well have just said that the "early bird doesn't get the worm." Yes, it does help knowing a lot of people, I will not argue against that point. But have you ever considered that the people they know know them? Huh?!? Think about it. If someone knows me well enough to have me on their list, then I know them well enough to know they don't know what they're doing. How could they? They just started! Yet countless New Guys are sent out of their offices to call on the very people who know the very thing that the salesman doesn't want anyone to know. So the friend, uncle, frat brother, Boy Scout leader, and Sunday school teacher does the respectful thing and grants the newbie an appointment. Recently one of my partners, Marty Jones, shared a great story with me. When he was fresh out of college, he granted his friend, a rookie life insurance salesman, a lunch appointment to discuss his needs for insurance. As lunch was wrapping up, the rookie smoothly slid his business card across the table saying, "Whenever you are ready to move forward with the insurance, just give me a call." Marty slid the card back to him saying, "I think I will be able to find you...seeing as though you're my roommate!!"

Here is a thought for you: Have you ever considered that those on your list may not appreciate the fact that you are using them to practice on? I used to work with a guy who banked on the fact that, since he knew "everybody," he was a shoe-in to get out of the gate quickly. The only problem was that "everybody" knew the guy had a job history the size of a phonebook. Not good. Against my better judgment, I gave him the benefit of the doubt. I asked him if he knew anybody at a prospective client's firm I was trying to call on. Smugly, he responded that not only did he know people there; his cousin Joe was an executive with the company. Armed with a C level relationship, we set an appointment to present our wares. As we pulled into the parking lot, I noticed one of their employees shoveling sand out of a wheelbarrow and spreading it around a flag pole. My colleague waved at him and said, "Hey, there's Joe." My immediate thought was, "Surely that isn't his cousin. After all he had said his cousin was a C level executive." Well he was. Evidently, the C he was referring to stood for Custodian! "Mr. Connected" lasted less than a year with us, and now I am sure he is hitting up those same people for his new venture. All right, since the friends and family plan is not the cure-all we were led to believe in, what do we do to get started? The answer: Anything and everything you can. I stress you because in the early going, you will be greeted with every war story of how your fellow colleagues became the successes they are today. Guess how much good that does you? Zero! What worked for them, may not work for you.

It's similar to a golf swing. The next time a golf event is on T.V., take a look at the swings of Jim Furyk and Adam Scott. Both of them have one goal: hit the ball to land as close to the hole as possible. Their swings couldn't be any more different. When Adam Scott swings, it's like poetry in motion, it looks effortless. When Jim Furyk swings, chiropractors get excited! Furyk twists and turns his body in a way that would cripple most mortal men. The results? As of this writing, Furyk has won close to $50 million during his PGA career. Adam is no slouch either, having pocketed around $25 million. The point is this:

# THERE ARE NO PICTURES ON A SCORECARD!

It's not how–it's how many. The same is true of your "sales swing." Take a look at your fellow colleagues. More than likely, they all have a different approach to how they sell. My advice for you is to take their best practices and find a way to work them into your style. As we will discuss in upcoming chapters, you have to be yourself and play to your strengths.

For me, it was smiling and dialing. For you, it may be civic groups or knocking on doors. No matter the method, the key to getting out of the blocks is: Massive

Activity. Remember the story of me catching the elbow? After reading that, many of you may think I was raised by a Marine Drill Sergeant or something. Not at all. The reason my dad didn't stop after delivering the blow is because he didn't even realize he had hit me. There was such a "yard sale" of elbows, knees, and feet that he probably couldn't distinguish between his own or mine. That is how it will be for you as you get started, if you start correctly. To move from survival to success, you have to come out hard and fast. It will feel as though you are doing the work of three men, which is partly true if you are talking about Moe, Larry, and Curly. Leave dignity and professionalism to the MBAs who are waiting tables, because like Clark Griswold's Cousin Eddie, they are still holding out for a management position. Don't sit there waiting for inspiration to strike you...it won't. You have to do the striking! Make a call, write a letter, knock on a door, join a Chamber, or solicit a past customer. Do something! Action creates results and getting results is the name of the game. This next statement may surprise you: Nobody cares what you did to get the customer. As long as it was moral and ethical, the actions you took to turn that prospect into a customer are long forgotten once the commission hits the books. Quick question: How much more do you get paid for selling a referral versus a cold call? Approximately? How 'bout zero! Your commission check doesn't discriminate, why should you? The money spends the same, doesn't it? As The New Guy, you will be encouraged by your colleagues to solely focus on getting referrals. In theory that sounds great, but in reality it doesn't work. When you are getting started, you don't have many customers to ask, and other people who will become great referral sources are waiting to see if you make it before they endorse you to their friends and associates. If I had waited for referrals to come my way, you would not be reading this. I would have fizzled out quickly because my referral base was extremely limited. Another reason you don't want to solely focus on referrals is because all referrals are not created equal. When a friend or colleague gives you a referral, you will feel obligated to work on it. Often they think they are doing you a favor by sending business your way, but as stated above, sometimes it turns out to be more of a hindrance than a help.

My dad has a statement that he drilled into me and my brothers growing up. It is simply, "Starting is half done." The hardest part of any project is getting started. I have noticed that my phone is much heavier when I first pick it up. After a few calls, it gets lighter and after a few more, it's effortless. I love the quote from Ralph Waldo Emerson, "That which we persist in doing becomes easier–not that the nature of the task has changed, but our ability to do has increased." Understanding the principles of Physics will help you tremendously in your sales career. Let me explain. Remember hearing that "things that are in motion, tend to stay in motion?" That is why it is vital for you to take action. The very act of starting an activity creates the momentum to continue it. When I sit down to make phone calls, I make sure to have everything I am going to need at my fingertips. Prospect files, notepads, extra pens and my headset are ready for action. I know that once I make that first call, I have to move immediately on to the next one, or else I will lose momentum. I will not check voice mail, email or my cell phone until I complete the calls that I need to. I highly encourage you to silence your cell phone and turn off your email when making calls. You don't want to have any distractions to keep you from doing what you need to do. Once again, you are paid to increase the top line of your organization. The sign up list for your office breakfast next week can wait, your sales calls can't!

I will never forget when I was given a referral customer by my colleague, Bruce Eades. I should have known something was awry when he was really happy to pass them along to me. I couldn't believe my good fortune! After all, I had been slaving away at trying to land new customers on my own, so to have one handed to me was greatly appreciated. My first order of business was to go out to their office and meet them. Those were the days before GPS–although where they were located, it probably wouldn't have mattered. The "office" was in their home, which resembled the estate of Fred Sanford (from "Sanford & Son" for those of you that were born after 1980). Briefcase in hand, I approached the door only to be greeted by not one, but two giant hound dogs! My gut told me to turn and run away. I should have listened to it. My new customer "greeted" me at the door with some profanity about how much she hates insurance...just what an insurance agent loves to hear. She pointed me toward the conference table, which resembled more of a kitchen table given the amount of uneaten meals left on it. She impolitely excused herself from the room while I unpacked my files. As I placed her policies in a neat stack right next to the burnt macaroni and cheese, I caught a glimpse of the hound dogs in the corner of my eye. Oh, how I wish the story ended there.

What I really wish is that they would have taken the advice of Bob Barker when he encouraged people to have their pets spayed or neutered. For some reason, to a hound dog my legs resemble a French Poodle. With a dog on each leg, what started out as an insurance meeting quickly became an outtake from the Discovery Channel.

This experience taught me several things–some of which have required counseling–but one thing I have remembered: All referrals are not created equal! Over time, my business has become more referral based, although I still to this day make cold calls. The reason? Because there are some accounts I want to land that I will never be referred into. It's nothing personal, it's just that right now, I don't have an "in" yet. So, I have a choice: I can wait around and hope I get an introduction, or I can create my own. I am not sure about your family, but mine eats at least three times a day. And remember: "Timid salesmen have skinny kids." Now stretch out your hammies, get down in a sprinters stance, and get out of the blocks! The fun has just begun!

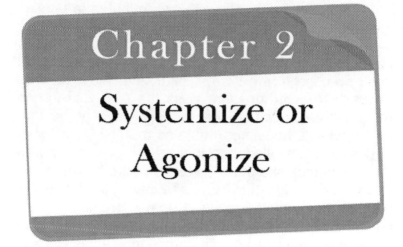

# Chapter 2

# Systemize or Agonize

*"Everyone has a plan...until they get hit in the mouth!"*

\- Mike Tyson

Pop quiz: You have exactly two minutes to provide me with a list of your top prospects for the upcoming twelve months. Can you do it? Put down the yellow pages, that doesn't count. Okay, you're a veteran, you don't "prospect" anymore; I hear you. All right, how about your record of client visits the past year in one minute...Go! Can't find that either? Could it be that you're having the same trouble as the guy Mark Twain described as "a blind man looking for a black cat in a dark room that isn't there"? We in the brethren of sales figure that our job is to leave the cave, kill something, drag it back to camp, and leave organization to somebody else. Yes, I am guilty of that as well, but I am amazingly organized when it comes to keeping track of my commission checks. Have you ever lost a commission check? Of course not! Then why are we so haphazard when it comes to systemizing and organizing the activities that directly lead to how many numbers are on that check? Because we forget how important those activities are.

Years ago, I figured out that certain actions always lead to results. The results may be good, bad, or ugly, but results came nonetheless. I then realized that in every sale there were certain events that always took place. At some point in time, I met my new customer for the first time. That meeting was preceded by some type of introduction. Perhaps it was a referral from a friend or customer, or it was generated from my calling them for an appointment. That initial meeting was followed by subsequent meetings which eventually led to a proposal. If the prospect said yes to the proposal: Voilà, I have a new customer! So being the math-

ematician that I am, I took out my abacus and came up
with this formula:

## X AMOUNT OF
## APPOINTMENTS
## BECOME Y AMOUNT
## OF PROPOSALS,
## WHICH LEAD TO
## Z AMOUNT OF NEW
## $$$$!

No, you can't get your money back for this book.
I've already spent it! Just because it's simple, don't
disregard it. Selling is not brain science...or is it rocket
surgery? Doesn't matter. What does matter is any
system beats no system.

The reason you and I need a system to our selling is
the same reason why you have heard of a Big Mac, but
not a Messy Burger. In my neck of the woods, the
greatest concoction of ground beef, lettuce, tomatoes,
and southern slaw is what we refer to as the Messy
Burger. A local burger joint by the name of Brad's Grill
makes the best burger you have ever eaten. The good
news is Brad himself cooks all the burgers. The bad news
is Brad himself cooks all the burgers. The reason you
have eaten a Big Mac and not a Messy Burger has
nothing to do with the quality of offering. Believe me, after
you partake in one of Brad's creations, you won't want to
visit the Golden Arches again. What McDonald's did that
Brad hasn't done, at least as of this writing, is create a
system that is duplicated all over the world every day. The
technical term is "franchising." I am not a Wharton

graduate, but breaking down franchising to its simplest form is:

1. Find out what works
2. Work what you found
3. Repeat process

Simple? Yes. Effective? Absolutely!

As the "New Guy," this chapter could not have come at a better time for you. I would encourage you to create a daily, weekly, monthly, and quarterly report that tracks your selling activities. This is not something that will go to your sales manager or boss. This is for you. The reason I encourage you to do it is because I did. I can't tell you how many times I would fill out the daily report and have virtually nothing of value to show for it. At least that is what I thought. What seemed as a worthless phone call gave me the information that would turn into a prospect. That prospect would, months or years later, turn into a client. The lesson is this: Without the initial "worthless" phone call, I would have never landed the client. If you don't track it, it's hard to keep making yourself do the grunt work that you have to do. Go to that client list I mentioned at the beginning of this chapter. You know, the one you couldn't find? Now, look at your newest client. How did you meet them? Whatever action, relationship, event, ad, website, or seminar that created the introduction can create another one. Look at #3 above. The only problem is you can't repeat a process you don't have.

Remember those "blue vest" days I mentioned earlier? You will have days when you will question why in the world you ever went into this business. That's when you need to pull out your reports and remind yourself that what you are doing today does pay dividends. We often get "sales amnesia" and forget that past success does guarantee future results!

To illustrate the importance of having a system, let me tell you the story of a guy I used to work with. For the sake of anonymity, let's call him Bill. Bill was a distributor for me in my air purification business several years ago. After the first couple of weeks, I noticed that despite tremendous potential, Bill had not been able to sell much product, so I figured I'd better find out what the problem was. I sent him a sales report that he was to fill out at the end of the week and send back to me. It listed the following three items: Appointments, Proposals, and Sales. Next to each item was a box. All Bill had to do was put a number in the box. I suspected something was amiss when I received his first report. It looked something like this:

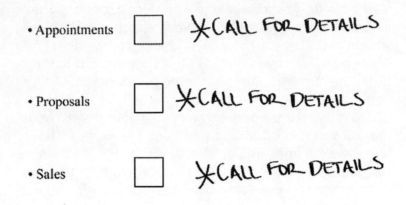

- Appointments ☐ *CALL FOR DETAILS

- Proposals ☐ *CALL FOR DETAILS

- Sales ☐ *CALL FOR DETAILS

Instead of filling out the boxes, he put an asterisk next to each one and wrote "call for details." I called. The details consisted of stories of what he would've, could've, and should've done. After several minutes of this, I finally stopped him and said, "Bill, the reason I made the boxes so small is so a story won't fit! I need a number!" The next paper I sent him was not a sales report...it was the classifieds.

I need to caution you. Creating a systematic approach to your daily activity will be a work in progress. Don't get overly rigid with your system. In sales, one of the best attributes you can have is flexibility. There will be many days when your plans get interrupted. The phone has a tendency to ring at the most inconvenient time. Your customer has a problem and you and only you can fix it. By the time you finish putting out his fire, half your day is gone. Finally, you can breathe again and you still have half a day to accomplish what you had initially set out to do.

## THIS IS THE EXACT MOMENT THAT WILL DETERMINE WHETHER YOU SUCCEED OR FAIL IN THE SALES GAME.

What you do with "left over" time is a huge determiner of success. You have the choice to fritter away the remaining half of your day doing non revenue producing tasks or you can shift gears immediately and get back on track. Often, we are tempted to reason with ourselves that since the day got off track, it has to stay off track. In a perfect world, we would be able to show up at the office and go from task to task without any interruptions. I hate to be the bearer of bad news, but you will never have a day without interruptions. That's why it is so important to have a system that you can put into action during the "left over" time. Like we talked about earlier in this chapter, if you have to enlist the services of the FBI to find your prospect list, you will never be able to take advantage of small increments of time. In a book shelf that is within arm's reach, I have a simple folder labeled, "follow up calls." In the folder are printed lead sheets that have all the pertinent information I need in order to make a prospect phone call: phone number, contact name, and any notes that are relevant. They are not arranged in any particular order, because when making prospect calls, it doesn't matter when you call them, only if you call them. I have tried every trick in the book: early morning calls, late afternoon calls, 11:59 a.m. calls...you name it, I have done it. Guess what? Your prospect doesn't care what time of day you call them; why should you? All that matters is doing the things you need to do consistently. The only way you will be able to do them consistently is by having a system in place to do them.

One of the great things about selling is that there is very little guess work when it comes to figuring out how you are doing. At the end of the day, month, quarter, and year, we get a report card. What is on that report card is measured not in A's or B's, but in dollars and cents. Getting a system and using that system consistently will help determine whether you make the Dean's List or get sent to the principal's office.

# Chapter 3

# Blocking and Tackling

*"Gentlemen...this is a football."*

- Vince Lombardi

One of the best statements I have ever heard on the subject of fundamentals comes from writer/ speaker John C. Maxwell. He says, *"Far too often we overestimate the results and underestimate the process that created them."* When talking about the importance of fundamentals, I am reminded of the late great football coach, Vince Lombardi. Legend has it that at the beginning of every training camp, Coach Lombardi would gather his team together, stand before them, hold up a football, and say, "Gentlemen, this is a football." Didn't they already know what a football was? Of course. They made their living throwing one, catching one, running with one, or tackling somebody who was doing any of the above. He was not "dumbing down" his coaching; he was reminding them of the basics.

Another favorite coach of mine is the legendary John Wooden. He won an unprecedented ten consecutive National Championships while coaching basketball for UCLA. He coached Hall of Famers like Lew Alcindor (Kareem Abdul Jabbar to the novice sports fan), and Bill Walton (who, in my opinion, intimidated his foes not so much with his playing, but with his savage red beard!). Coach Wooden would spend an entire practice showing his players how to properly put on their socks. Why? Because improperly worn socks lead to blisters, and no matter how good you are, you can't play with blisters. So, what are the "socks" of sales and how can we make sure we are wearing them properly? If you read ten different books on the subject of sales, you may get ten different opinions on what makes up the fundamentals of our profession. I don't think it's that complicated. I have always been one to tell you the time and not how to make a watch. If you wanted a more technical book, you came to the wrong place...of course if you have read this far, you know that already. No matter what you are selling, it basically comes down to three vital skills:

#1 Prospecting

#2 Qualifying the Prospect

#3 Creating and Maintaining Client Relationships

I know; you assumed #3 was going to be "Closing the Deal." It's not. If you Qualify correctly, the "close" is very anti-climactic. Yes, I know that "coffee's for closers," but I also know that if you are one to jump right to the close, then your business relationships will be very similar to when I dated my wife. Our relationship was fast and furious. I was fast...she was furious!

I'm not sure why so many of us want to jump ahead of the basics. Maybe it's the same reason we don't read instruction manuals. A few years ago, we bought my son a street hockey set for Christmas. I should have known I was in for a challenge when the box said "some assembly required." That statement never quite tells the whole story. Kind of like an insurance policy- the bold print giveth and the fine print taketh away! Although I never played hockey (because my name is too easy to pronounce), I do know what a net is supposed to look like. The result of what I put together looked more like a medieval torture device than a hockey net. There were screws sticking out all over the place, and the net looked like something on *Deadliest Catch*. My wife Wendy could overhear my struggle and came to the rescue. You can guess her first question: "Did you read the instructions?" I gave the answer that any red-blooded American man would: "Of course not!" She gave me that look that every husband has seen...some of us more than others. In less than five minutes, she had the net put together and I had some more eggnog.

Now back to Selling. Think of a sale like a baseball diamond. First Base is Prospecting. Second Base is Qualifying the Prospect. Third Base is Developing the Relationship. Once you "round third," scoring is inevitable. There is a reason they call it "First Base." It's where you are supposed to start. Unfortunately, not everybody starts there. I had the pleasure of coaching my son Tanner when he played T-Ball. If you haven't been to a T-Ball game in a while, I encourage you to do so. Coaching T-Ball players is very similar to herding cats. They are much more concerned about the postgame snacks than they are the score. One thing you are guaranteed to see at least once a game is a kid attempting to run the bases the wrong way. They hit the ball and then the excitement of the moment takes over and off they go...to third base! The parents and coaches howl with laughter and try to instruct them that they are going the wrong way. What happens? They interpret the crowd noise as encouragement to keep running–so they run even faster–the wrong way!! I think we even had a couple of backwards home runs. Now, here is where this example applies to you.

## THE ONLY TIME IT'S FUNNY TO RUN THE WRONG WAY IS IN T-BALL!!!

Countless New Guys want to score so badly that they end up skipping some of the bases. The Third Base Coach has the "Stop Sign" up, but they pay it no attention. They round third only to be greeted by the Catcher who has had the ball for awhile. They stop, jump, slide, beg, and plead with the Catcher...but to no avail. Two words: You're Out!! They come back to the bench (office) and explain to their teammates (co-workers) that the ump (customer) made a terrible call. Sound familiar? To prove this point, all you have to do is look at the career of Ichiro Suzuki. For years he has led the Major Leagues in number of hits. Not coincidentally, he usually leads in stolen bases and runs scored. The more singles he hits (Prospecting), the more opportunities he has to steal second base (Qualifying). From second base, third base is not that far away (Relationship Building). From there, scoring runs is easy. But don't forget...it all started with base hits. Base hits win ball games and sales.

Maybe baseball isn't your game and you are more of a weekend warrior on the links. Well, if you are a golfer, you have no doubt heard the cliché "You drive for show, you putt for dough." I play a fair amount of golf, though not much lately because my ball retriever is being re-gripped. I can tell you that no matter how good a putter you are, you can't score if your tee shots are in the woods. Selling is much the same. So many times we are focused on the end result and not on the process that gets us there.

A few years ago I got the itch to learn the guitar. My brothers had already been playing for a few years and when we would get together, inevitably our visit would turn into a jam session. Our family would gather around and they would strum out some "sing alongs." The Eagles, Bon Jovi and John Denver certainly never intended their music to be sung like that! During these sessions all I had to offer was my vocal talent and occasionally some work on the tambourine. It was killing me not being able to play along with them! So, I bought a guitar and began my quest to master the six string. The first thing I did was went out and bought a chord book. I was told that most songs are played in three chords: G, C & D. The book had pictures showing exactly how to position your hand and how to place your fingers in the correct position on the guitar. What it didn't tell me is that after about five minutes of strumming Margaritaville, the strings would feel like razor blades. My finger tips throbbed in pain! I called my brothers asking if they had experienced this same pain while learning. They were both in agreement. The pain of developing calluses was something every guitar player had to endure. There were no shortcuts. Hour after hour I pressed my aching fingers on the fret board, hoping that something resembling a tune would come out. I probably need to take this time to apologize to my wife, kids and the neighbor dog for the horrific sounds I subjected them to. Finally, my fingers toughened up and I learned all the chords I would ever need: G, C & D. Now, if you want to hear me play a song in any of those, I'm golden...if not, pick another song!

There have been many sales careers cut short because they didn't build calluses. The first time it hurt a little bit, they threw in the towel and decided to play a different instrument. You need to remember that fundamentals aren't necessarily fun.

# Chapter 4

# Eskimo Hunting

*"Do it! Move it! Make it happen! No one ever sat their way to success."*

- H. Jackson Brown

The best closers first have to have someone to close. Don't believe me? Put the book down and go into your break room. More than likely there is a "closer" in there scarfing down his third donut of the morning who swears that he can sell ice cream to Eskimos. Only problem is he can't find any Eskimos!

An ancient Chinese secret says: "The journey of a thousand miles begins with a single step." And you thought you couldn't find any good stuff in fortune cookies? I believe that the journey of a thousand sales begins with a single call. As I discussed earlier, you can memorize your script, master every objection, and be the king of closes, but if you don't have someone to sell to, you will not make it in this business. My mentor and business partner, Bruce, has a statement he preaches to all of us in our office. It is simply, "Pipeline equals power!" If your pipeline of prospects is full, everything else takes care of itself. How many times have you worked a prospect, closed the deal, collected the money, and celebrated the victory...only to be hit with the realization that you just lost your best and, unfortunately, only prospect? It's bad enough to be hit with that reality after making a sale. How about after not making the sale? It's in moments like these where you suddenly start making sure your wardrobe matches with a blue vest. I have found that the only thing that softens the blow of losing an account is if you have another one right behind it to work on. That being the case, how can we make sure our pipeline is constantly full? By constantly working on it.

If you are inconsistent in your prospecting activities, your sales numbers will follow suit. Going back to

Chapter two, if you don't create a system early on in your sales career for consistent prospecting, odds are you will never create one. As the New Guy, your entire work day is consumed with new business activities because you don't have any existing business to service. As your business grows, more of your time is taken up with the day to day servicing of your accounts. If you're not careful, servicing your existing clientele will take up all of your time. You will be rushing around putting out fires, and at the end of the week you will look back and realize you had no time to do any prospecting. We need to view prospecting activities like we do any other daily task. I don't particularly like shaving every day, but unless I change careers to selling Birkenstock sandals, then shaving it is. So we have established the fact that prospecting is a must.

## NOW *WHAT* IS IT AND MORE IMPORTANTLY, *WHY* AND *WHEN* DO YOU DO IT?

At its root, prospecting is simply: finding people who will buy from you. If you go through your customer files, you will discover that at one point in time, that customer was a stranger to you. They may have been a name on a list, an unknown attendee at a function, or a strange voice on the other end of a phone. Regardless of the origin, you found them. The only question you need to ask yourself is: "What did I do to find them?" If you can answer that, you know the "what" of prospecting. Remember, your "what" may be different than my "what." Don't get caught up in debating the techniques of prospecting. If you hate cold calling...don't do it. Find something else that works for you. The numbers are all that matter. If you are consistently getting in front of new prospects, keep doing it. If you aren't, then "Houston, we have a problem." You have to develop your own style of selling. Organizations that "cookie cut" their sales reps will create a couple of things. One is high turnover; the other is a sales force of robots. In my opinion, the more structured of an environment a company creates, the less creative their people will be. One of my partners, Steve Heinen, has never made a cold call...ever. He gets his business by being an educational resource for companies throughout the state of Georgia. Over the years, he has positioned himself as one of the authorities on Workers Comp law. In many cases, he knows more about the rules and regulations than most Attorneys. Prospects call him. Wouldn't that be nice? Now what would happen if Steve were forced to sit down every day and bang out cold calls? I will tell you. He wouldn't still be in the insurance business. Instead of "dialing for dollars" he invests his time in education, and in turn has become a trusted advisor to his clients who in turn refer him to other companies. I know what you're thinking: "That's great for Steve, but what about me?!?" What about you? What can you do? Much of the what of prospecting is trial and error.

For years I have tried going to various business functions hoping to meet some potential clients or make some new acquaintances. I am embarrassed to say that on most occasions, I leave within the first few minutes. Those that know me would be shocked to know that in some social situations, I clam up like a wallflower. After several failed attempts I realized my problem: if I am not in control of the environment or know someone there, I get extremely self conscious and start looking for the exit. So I had a decision to make...either take Valium before going to one of those functions, or figure out a different strategy. I gave it some thought and came up with a new plan. If I could just have a "wing man," I would be fine. Enter my buddy Scott Brown. Scott can walk into any environment and instantly act like he owns the place. Now when I go to a function out of my comfort zone, I make sure Scott comes with me. We work the room...together. Problem solved. I am now able to make new business contacts at high level functions, all because I was willing to acknowledge my fear of going solo and reached out to a friend for help. We both leave with new contacts and potential clients. Classic win-win scenario.

Why prospect? To create new sales, you have to meet new people. As basic as that sounds, I am amazed at how often we argue with it. For some reason we over analyze our profession and think that sales just happen. They don't. There is nothing mystical about sales or success for that matter. Success is something you do. It is not done for you. This may not be a popular position to take, seeing as how millions of people are hoping that success is going to somehow be attracted to them by this new "secret" method the masses are buying into. The only thing you will find by sitting around waiting is a commission check that is mediocre at best. How do I know this? Because I have had them. I still hold the record at my office for the smallest commission check...twenty-eight cents. It's bad when the stamp on the envelope is worth more than the check in the envelope! The numbers on your commission statement will mirror the numbers of your prospecting. What you sow, so shall you reap! That was written a long time ago, and it is just as true today as when it was written. As you can tell, I am a big believer in keeping records of my sales activity. I am not one to promote paperwork for paperwork's sake, but it is painfully true that if my numbers are low on my sales report, then the numbers on my paycheck will follow suit.

Knowing why to prospect is important, but the bigger question is when? To answer that, let's look at another key ingredient to succeeding in sales: Knowing your sales cycle. How long does it take for you to close a new account? This will vary depending on what you sell for a living. If you sell products over the phone, you may be able to close a new account in a matter of minutes. If you sell business insurance (like I do) it can take years to close certain accounts. Understanding your sales cycle will help you decide when to prospect. The prospects you are closing today are a direct result of the prospecting you did X days, months, or years ago. So if you want to close new sales X days, months, or years from now, you'd better be prospecting right now.

You may have heard the adage that "defense wins championships." That is only partly true. You can have the best defense in the world, but if you don't score enough points, it's all for naught. Think of prospecting as being on offense. Now look at your daily routine.

How much time is being devoted to playing offense versus playing defense? If you find yourself straightening your desk, organizing paperclips, checking your voicemail...again, then you my friend are playing defense. Playing defense when you're supposed to be playing offense is bad enough, but what's worse is when we play "prevent" defense. If you are a football fan, you know what I'm talking about. If you aren't, let me explain. When a team is ahead, it is customary for them to revert to a "bend but don't break" defensive scheme. They have fewer guys rush the quarterback and focus on not giving up a big play. Guess what happens? They get sloppy, and more times than not, the other team marches down the field and scores. The only thing that it prevents is the team from winning. If you find yourself waiting for your customers to call you, you are in "prevent" mode. Your defense, like your offense, must be played aggressively. Call your customers. Better yet, take them to lunch. If you back up and wait, guess who marches down the field? Your competitors.

As a sixth grader, I was the point guard for our school's basketball team. We lived in a very small town in rural Louisiana, and it was always difficult to round up enough players to field a team. As our team captain (which is an easy title to claim when you are the only one who can dribble a ball), I took it upon myself to recruit some more talent. I started with my neighbor, Warren. He immediately rejected my offer to join the team, stating that he was a horrible player and we would regret having him on the hardwood. I persuaded him anyway. So with a pair of short shorts that would make Larry Bird proud and some beat up Chuck Taylors, Warren made his debut. I should have listened to him. What tipped me off was when I brought the ball down the court and watched in horror as Warren proceeded to play the most tenacious defense I had ever seen. He was on his guy like stink on a monkey! The only problem was...we were on offense! Now before you bust on poor ol' Warren, ask yourself: "Am I playing defense when I should be playing offense?"

I remember getting some great advice years ago on the importance of always having new business to close: even if you retain ninety percent of your clients, but add no new business, in five years your business will be half of what it is today. Think about that for a minute. A ninety percent retention rate for your customers is a very good number, but without new business you are going backwards.

Have you noticed that anything of value has to be worked on consistently? Whether it's your physical fitness, spiritual fitness, or financial fitness, consistency is the key. The same is true of prospecting. Just remember:

## THE CALL YOU
## *DON'T* MAKE
## *CAN'T* HELP YOU.

So pick up the phone, attend the function, knock on the door. One of my favorite Bible Verses is Matthew 7:7. It's written in red, so that means it comes straight from the source: "Ask and it shall be given. Seek and ye shall find. Knock and the door shall be opened unto you." What's the common thread throughout that verse? Look at the bold print. ASK. Success in prospecting all comes down to consistent asking. My youngest daughter Kylee has it all figured out. She will make a great salesperson someday. She and her big sister Cameron had asked for something and the answer was no. After they stormed up the stairs in a huff, I overheard Kylee consoling Cameron. She said, "Don't worry. All we have to do is just keep asking Daddy and he will eventually say yes." And just think, she hasn't even read my book yet!

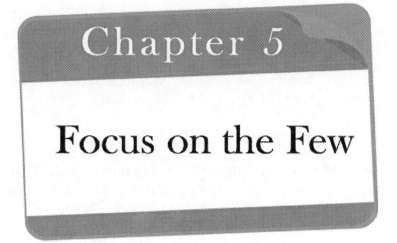

# Chapter 5

# Focus on the Few

*"The more you know, the less you need."*

- Yvon Chouinard

Now that your prospecting activities are in full swing, you may be asking, "What do I do with all these prospects?" My answer to that: Eliminate them. "What?! I just bought into making calls, attending functions, building my pipeline, and now you want me to get rid of them?" Yes, but not all of them.

Qualifying prospects is a huge component to sales success. We need to realize that just because someone will meet with me it doesn't mean I should do business with them. When I started my career in insurance, I met a sales trainer named Roger Sitkins. He teaches that every time you meet with a prospect, you need to ask yourself, "Why should I do business with them?" Rarely does a salesperson ever ask that. In most cases, we are just happy to have someone to meet with, and we look for every reason to justify moving forward with the sales process. I have found that the sooner you eliminate a prospect, the better. Sitkins also has a statement that has stuck with me ever since I first heard it. He says, "The best day to lose a sale is the first day." Think about that. Far too often we meet with a prospect, go back to our office, and begin the process of putting together a proposal for their business. Depending on your industry, this process can be very time consuming and very expensive. We jump through all the hoops, take the time of our staff, and exhaust resources on the prospect...only to find out at the last minute that his current provider is his brother-in-law! We never had a ghost of a chance to sell the prospect anything. All we did was waste our time and further delay our next sale. To prevent this, we need to make sure that the person we are meeting with is indeed a true prospect.

It has taken me years to move away from prospecting to the masses. For most of my career, I bought into the concept that selling is a numbers game. I won't argue the fact that if you call on enough people you will create sales. But at what expense? The amount of time I have wasted on dead end prospects is mind numbing. Again, part of being the New Guy is cutting your teeth on deals that don't go your way. Don't beat yourself up for striking out on a few here and there...there is no substitute for experience. Just make sure you don't keep repeating the same mistakes. Take a look at your prospect list. Hopefully after reading Chapter two you have created one. If not...put the book down and do so. Now, ask yourself the following two questions:

Question #1: How many prospects are on your list?

Question #2: How many on that list could pick your name out of a lineup?

Here's the deal. I spent years focused on Question #1. I felt a sense of security by having a large prospect list to call on. If prospect A said no, simply move to prospect B. I spent very little time on Question #2.

## WHAT I CREATED WAS A PROSPECT BASE THAT WAS A MILE WIDE BUT ONLY AN INCH DEEP.

Year after year I would call the same prospects only to be met with the news that they had already made their decision for the upcoming year, and unfortunately, it didn't include me. Finally, one day I asked myself: "Why am I finding out about these decisions after they have already been made?" The answer was humbling. The reason I was always a day late and a dollar short was because, to the prospect, I was simply a vendor who called them once a year. If I had time, I would maybe drop them a letter or two throughout the year, but nothing of any value and certainly nothing consistent. So when the subject of buying insurance came up, hopefully I would catch them at just the right time to have a chance at getting in the game. My livelihood depended completely on timing. For that to work, I had to have a huge prospect base and hope that they answered the phone when I made my annual call. I'm not sure if you have noticed, but over the last several years people are getting better at avoiding phone calls. This truth hit me when I found myself screening calls. When my office phone rings, I look at the number on my caller ID, and if I don't recognize it, I let it go to voice mail. Guess what? Your prospects do the exact same thing. In light of this, my days of being a highly paid telemarketer were over. There had to be a better way. I had to change my approach. I needed new ideas, new strategies. I had to come to grips with the fact that what worked in the past would not work in the present or the future. This was not easy. It's hard to abandon practices that have produced results. I guess part of it is pride. I had built my business on being a "Cold-Calling Cowboy," and I was proud of it. What I didn't plan on was that technology would make my old method of prospecting obsolete. I could either buck against it or double my efforts–which would basically mean getting thrown into twice as many "voice jails"– or use technology as a tool. I chose the latter. As of this writing, I have reduced my prospect list from several hundred "suspects" to seventy-five potential clients. Instead of "shot-gunning" my message across the fruited plain, I now focus on delivering value to the seventy-five prospect companies on a regular basis. My prospects get "touched" once a month at a minimum. I have used online resources such as LinkedIn to research my prospects information, like where they went to college, organizations they belong to, etc. All in the name of focusing more attention on fewer prospects. The results? I have had more new business appointments in the past six months than I have had in the past five years, and just last month I landed a new client which produced revenue that exceeded my new business goal for the entire year! Less Is More! The more time and thought you can put into fewer people, the more true opportunities you will create. This philosophy is counterintuitive. We learn at an early age that, after all, there are always "more fish in the sea." We are taught that to minimize risk, we need to increase our odds by spreading our risk.

While that technique may help you at the tables in Vegas, it doesn't help you land new clients, or catch fish for that matter. Last year, my town hosted the "Super Bowl of Bass Fishing," the FLW Championship. It brought professional anglers from all over the country. The winner, Kevin Hawk, had a different strategy than the rest of his competitors. To increase his odds of winning, he actually moved to the area from California and rented from a family that owned a lake home. Sun-up to sun-down, he fished that lake. He learned every inch of it. He didn't hope to find bass, he knew exactly where they would be. He knew his prospects. His strategy worked. He won $600,000. Not sure where you live, but around here that is pretty good money.

Once we determine who our prospects are, we have to be honest with ourselves and ask the tough questions: Why are they meeting with us? Do we have anything to offer them that they don't already have? Other than the person we are meeting with, who are the key players involved? I learned the lesson of that last question the hard way. Early in my insurance career, I was working on a very large prospect. At the time, it was by far the largest deal I had ever worked on. During our first meeting I asked the prospect if she was the decision maker. She answered, "Yes, I will make the decision." I assumed she was telling the truth and proceeded with putting together a proposal. Everything was falling into place for me. The prospect even went so far as to call me the night before we were to meet and gave me the competitor's proposal. I couldn't believe my good fortune! I had inside information! I knew exactly what the other agent had proposed, so all I had to do was revise my numbers and the order was mine...or so I thought. To bolster my chances, I brought two of my colleagues with me to the meeting. With all the confidence and swagger of the Three Musketeers, we walked into the meeting. Shortly thereafter we would walk out...like the Three Stooges! Apparently my "decision maker" turned out to be nothing more than a glorified receptionist. The real decision maker, the owner, had already met with another agent and signed the contract the day before!! Moral of the story: Unless your prospect is the CEO or owner, there is always someone else involved in making the decision.

Once you determine that you are meeting with the right who, and you are comfortable with the why, it's time to make sure you have the correct what. This is where honesty comes in. The fact of the matter is, not everyone should be your customer. As the New Guy, this is a tough pill to swallow. Often we try to fit square pegs into round holes. You can sell the finest quality aluminum siding in the world, but if your prospect lives in a brick house, you are wasting your time. I have found that prospects actually appreciate your honesty and hold you in higher regard when you are willing to walk away from a potential deal because it's not the right fit. Just because it doesn't fit now doesn't mean it won't fit later. If you remember one thing from this chapter, make it this next statement: Never burn a bridge. Situations can and will change over time. The rude CFO you met with at ABC company probably won't be there in a couple of years. So, don't give up on doing business with ABC. Just wait until Mr. Poopy Pants gets fired, then go back and get the deal.

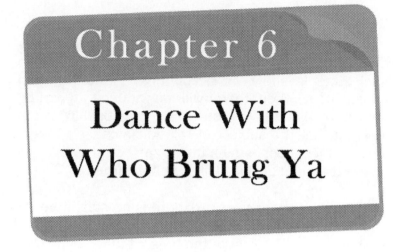

# Chapter 6

# Dance With Who Brung Ya

"All things being equal, people buy from people they like."

- Jeffrey Gitomer

How many classes have you taken on Business relationships? I am guessing none. Why is it that so much time is spent on accounting, marketing, and management when there will be nothing to count, market, or manage if there is no relationship? I am guessing that the subject of relationships isn't taught because most people think that it can't be. I disagree. I believe that relationship skills can be learned.

Just like any relationship, there is no substitute for time. Sometimes you can hit it off immediately with a new customer, but most of the time...it takes time. One thing I have found is that some customers are easier to get close to than others. The more you like someone, the more time you will want to spend with them. These relationships are fairly easy to maintain; they are also easy to take for granted. If you're not careful, you will find yourself spending far too much time trying to get new people to like you instead of spending time with the people that already do.

## IF SOMEONE DOESN'T LIKE YOU, THEY WILL NOT BUY FROM YOU...*PERIOD*.

You can try every pitch in your arsenal, but if someone doesn't like you, you will never build a relationship with them. The sooner you realize this, the better. Just remember back to high school. The girl that wouldn't give you the time of day (even though you had the coolest Camaro and a stylish mullet) still doesn't like you! It's the same with sales. Haven't you been approached by a salesperson who fire hoses you with all the great things their product and service does and how much they look forward to doing business with you, and all you can think about is what you are going to eat for lunch? No matter what that salesperson says or does is not going to matter. You don't like them and you probably never will. Now, the painful truth that we in the sales game must face is that to certain people, we are "that guy." Save yourself the time, money, and heartache and move on. For some reason, we sometimes confuse persistence with stalking. Quick question: Do you have more restraining orders than customer orders? If so, you might be a stalker. Every second you waste on the person that will never like you is time you could have been investing with those that will.

One of the knocks on salespeople is that after we have closed the sale, we move on to the next target and totally forget about the new customer we have just brought into the fold. Think about your newest customer. What did you do to win the account? Something tipped the scales your way. What was it? Superior product? Pricing? Timing? A referral? It is important for us to realize that until we build an airtight relationship with that new customer, whatever got us into the account can get us out of the account. If it was your superior price, what's going to happen when your competitor shows up with better pricing than yours? I will answer that question for you: Your customer will become an ex-customer. What if your superior product becomes yesterday's news? Again, same answer as above. We need to put forth as much effort into building the relationship with that customer as we did in trying to win the account. If you are married, think back to when you were dating your spouse. I can guarantee you that you did things to win his or her affection that you haven't done since. Guys, how often do you go shopping with your wife? Answer: "Uh...never." Exactly. Next question: "How often did you go shopping with her when you were dating?" Answer: "As often as she wanted to." I am now telling on myself. The first date I had with my wife, I actually took her to...are you ready for this...an art museum! I did lose my "Man Card" for a little while after that. Can you imagine? My appreciation for art ranges between a Velvet Elvis and the dogs playing poker! Why would I do that? Because I was trying anything and everything to impress her. We do the same thing when trying to win a new customer. We pull out all the stops, promise the moon, compliment their lousy golf game...all in the name of landing a new customer. Once landed, too often we look for our next conquest. We need to make certain that our customers don't feel like the lyricist that penned the classic Jermaine Jackson song...check that...only Jermaine Jackson song, "Why don't you do what you do when you did what you did to me." And yes, it's on my iTunes.

I am an insurance agent. There aren't many professions that are more commoditized than mine. There are agencies on every street corner that can offer my customers a similar product or service, but there is only one where they can get me and my team. Now when I say "me and my team," that's exactly what I mean. Let me explain. My clients don't just get the products and services we offer, they get us. They get our relationship. While they may call Tricia to tell her to add a new vehicle to their insurance, they also catch her up with what is going on with their kids. Now that's a relationship. To reach that level of relationship, you have to change your mindset from one of transactional to relational. Yes, we do all the transactions that are required, but we do them all while building the relationship. Far too many people rush through their day getting everything done, only to find their desk is just as piled up as it was when they started the day.

Relationships can't be rushed. How does it feel when you are talking to someone and you know the entire time that all they can think about is getting you off the phone so they can do something "really" important? You have to realize that in your customers' eyes, you only have one important customer...them. I hate it when I go to a store to buy something, money in hand, I get to the cash register to pay them, and they make me wait so that they can answer the phone and talk to someone who might buy. Has that ever happened to you?

My Dad and I were riding around one day and were nearly hit by an oncoming car. We swerved, blew our horn, and I think I even gestured to the guy that he was #1. When we came to a stop my Dad was visually shaken. I asked him, "Dad, are you alright?" He said, "No, son. To think that I just almost lost the person I love the most in this world really shakes me up." "Wow Dad, that really means a lot to hear you say that." He replied, "Son, I wasn't talking about you."

Mary Kay Ash, the founder of Mary Kay cosmetics, was famous for telling her saleswomen that they need to realize that every one of their customers is wearing an invisible sign that says: "Make me feel important." How do you make your customers feel important? A couple of years ago I started calling, texting, or emailing my clients on their birthday. I can't take credit for the idea; I have to give it to my financial advisor, Tommy Turner. For years, he has called me on my birthday. Of course, he should. After all, I have entrusted unto his care tens, if not hundreds of dollars! Do you contact your customers on their birthdays? We all say we want to have close relationships with our customers, but we don't take the necessary steps to get close to them. Guess who calls them on their birthday? Their family and close friends. What if their (insert your title here) called them? Better question is, what if your competitor calls and you don't?!?

Volumes of books have been written on how to serve customers, but I think you really only need one...The Bible. Some call it the Golden Rule, and although it was written centuries ago, it is still as true today as it was then. Simply "Do unto others as you would have them do unto you." A few years ago, I was sitting in our fireplace room in my reading chair with a fresh cup of coffee about to crack open a new book I had just bought on customer service. My son had other ideas on how I was going to spend the afternoon. He wanted to throw the football, and the only thing standing in the way of that was me reading a book. He took one look at the title of the book and said: "Dad, I can save you a bunch of time. Just be nice." I asked him: "Is that it?" "Yep, that's it. Be really nice to your customers and they will be nice to you. Now, let's go play some football!" Well said.

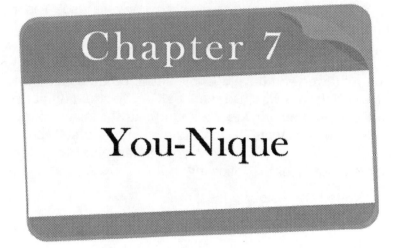

# Chapter 7

# You-Nique

*"I'm good enough, smart enough and doggonit...people like me."*

- Stuart Smalley

What makes you different than everyone else? Yes, I know...Your mom told you that you are special and "just like a snowflake: completely unique and there is nobody in the world like you." If your mom didn't tell you that then you have a whole set of other issues that I can't help you with. But seriously, if we are all unique individuals then why do we sound like the exact same person to prospects? I don't know what you sell, but I would be willing to bet that your sales pitch includes some if not all of the following:

"Nobody beats our prices"

"We have the best service"

"Our people are the best in the business"

"Our experience is what sets us apart"

"We focus on the customer"

Don't get me wrong. The above are all important as they relate to business, but guess what your competitor is saying? Yep...the exact same thing! News flash: One of you is wrong! You can't both have the best price, best service, and best people.

I remember when I had to come to grips with the fact that in some situations, I wasn't the "best." I was a sophomore in high school and it happened on a football field in DeKalb, Illinois. The score was 44–0 at the half. Our opponents scored on all of their possessions, and unfortunately, all of ours. They returned three punts for touchdowns, ran back an interception for another score, and during the short time they had the ball on offense, they served us with a hearty helping of the wishbone...all resulting in touchdowns. It was ugly. As I was going into the locker room at half time, I walked past our cheerleaders who tried their best to cheer us up with such proclamations as "We're #1," and something about "We can't be beat." I asked our cheer captain, if she had taken the time to notice the scoreboard, because if she had she would have obviously noticed that indeed we can be beat...The only number that represents what we were displaying on the gridiron was not #1, but #2!

One of the keys to succeeding in sales is to find situations where you–and only you–are the "best." You have to find scenarios where the deck is stacked in your favor; where your unique product/service offering is not only the best option, but the only option. I have heard and read many experts on sales, and there is no consensus on what a good closing ratio should be. I have an idea of what it should be: How about one hundred percent? Hear me out on this. Why would you want to compete if you're not confident that you will prevail? I don't know about you, but if you added up all the commission dollars that I have earned from finishing second, it would come to the grand total of...zero!! Far too often we opt to play on a level playing field. I will let you in on a little secret: There ain't no such thing. Somebody has the advantage. If you have to ask yourself who it is, it's not you! It's like the quote from the movie Rounders: "If you can't spot the sucker at the table in the first five minutes, you are the sucker!"

Our success will dramatically increase when we stop playing on their field. Let me explain. Have you ever heard of "home field advantage?" In the world of sports, the home team wins the majority of the time. In fact, in the NFL between 1999–2002, home teams averaged five points more than the visitors. Why is this? While the fan support certainly helps, it's more than that. One reason is that the home team doesn't have to travel. They can sleep in their own bed the night before the game instead of a hotel room. The home team locker rooms are also set up to give them an advantage. Word has it that the former home of the Boston Celtics, the Boston Garden, was a nightmare for the visiting team. The locker room was cramped, had bad lighting, and the plumbing was less than stellar. The fact remains that playing on someone else's turf is more difficult than playing on your own.

Now, how does this come into play in the sales game? Here's how: Your ability to control where you do your selling will have an impact on your results. At the least, you need to get your prospect to a neutral site. Get them out of their office! Preferably to yours, or somewhere where you have the advantage. One thing that I have had great success with is hosting seminar luncheons. We will bring in experts to speak on a variety of subjects that our prospects/clients are interested in. The beauty of having clients and prospects sitting at the same table is that your client actually does the selling for you! At some point during the luncheon your client and prospect will talk business and inevitably the prospect will ask about you. It's at this point that your client closes the deal for you! Again, the more you can sell on your turf, the better.

This style of selling takes some strategy and a willingness to take risks. I will never forget the time that one of my partners and I "rolled the dice" on a prospecting idea. Bruce walked into my office with that "I've got a great idea" look in his eye. One thing I knew for certain was that, in order for the idea to make us money, it was first going to cost us money. A little detail I failed to mention was that at this point in our business...we had no money! Here is what we did: We drafted an email to some key clients and large prospects inviting them to an all expense paid trip to visit our corporate headquarters in Orlando. They would learn more about our company and how we do business, go to dinner, play golf, and have a great time. With great anticipation–actually fear–we hit "send." Instantly, we had a response from one of our new key clients. At that point, we only insured part of that client's operations and were trying pick up the rest of their account. Long story short: We had a great trip, got to know the client much better than we ever would have at his office, and over time we were fortunate enough to pick up the rest of their account. It all goes back to a single email invitation and the willingness to invest in a client relationship.

This next question might be the best in the entire book.

## WHEN WAS THE *LAST* TIME YOU DID SOMETHING FOR THE *FIRST* TIME?

Read it again. I'm sure you have heard the statement "insanity is doing the same thing over and over and expecting different results." My buddy Jeff Stowe has a better one, "If you are banging your head against a wall, eventually you need to realize that it hurts!" I will be the first to admit that I have done my fair share of "head banging." I have thought that maybe if I bang my head a little softer or perhaps add some padding to the wall that it won't hurt. A few concussions later I have to come to grips with the fact that my current strategy isn't working. Now, I am not advocating change for change's sake. If you are experiencing success, you are doing something right. Don't stop doing it. But, to reach higher levels you will have to start doing new things and stop doing some of the things that have brought you to where you are.

I remember my first sales slump. At the time I was earning my stripes selling newspapers door to door. If you haven't had a slump yet, let me prepare you. You will question yourself, your products, your company, and your decision to enter this profession. I have said many times that when I was the New Guy, I only thought about quitting twice...Twice a day, every day! I was in rough shape. I actually borrowed some of my dad's old motivational tapes. Zig Ziglar and Earl Nightingale became my refuge. I was nearing the end of my rope when I got an idea. For every newspaper subscription we sold, part of the proceeds went to support a local children's home for the disabled. What if I could show my prospects just who their subscription dollars were helping? I went to the children's home and picked up every brochure they had. My prospects could now see who they were helping. My presentation changed from talking about the features of the paper to showing the benefits of their subscription dollar. Slump over.

Go back to the beginning of this chapter. How are you different? Still don't have an answer? Looks like we have more work to do.

Is there anything about you or your company that sets you apart from the competition?

If you can't answer that question quickly, guess what? Your customers can't either! The most unique business person I know comes from a profession few would ever describe as being creative. He is my kids' orthodontist, Dr. Ron Wilson. This guy is incredible! As a new orthodontist in our town, one of the first things he did was reach out to the dental community. He put on a golf outing for local dentists at one of the most prestigious country clubs in the Atlanta area. Not only did he rent out the whole club for the day, he chartered a tour bus to transport the dentists there and back and picked up the entire tab. Guess who the area dentists are referring their patients to now? I had one of them tell me that prior to Dr. Wilson, the biggest "thank you" he ever got from an orthodontist was a cold ham at Christmas. Hmmm...cold ham or golf outing? Which do you think paid bigger dividends? Now on to his patients (i.e. customers). It's hard to walk around this town and not see a kid proudly wearing a "Got Tin?" t-shirt. As a take on the "Got Milk?" campaign, he gives every kid that visits his office a t-shirt in their favorite color, and if they wear it to future appointments, they get tokens that they can turn into prizes. To top it off, he has gone above and beyond to endear himself to the ones that really matter...the moms. When they bring their tin-wearing kids for a checkup, instead of sitting in a waiting room reading an outdated People magazine, they head for the nail salon. That's right. He has put in a nail salon to pamper the moms! They can get a mani-pedi while they wait, all compliments of Dr. Wilson. Pretty good, huh? It's no wonder that in the midst of the great recession, his business is booming. As you can see from the picture below, the Peacock family has done their part to help. ☺

I think one of the obstacles to creativity is that all of our lives we have been encouraged to "fit in." No one wants to be a loner. We crave acceptance from our peers, and the end result of that desire is that we all end up looking, sounding, and being...the same. Marketing guru Seth Godin came up with the notion of being a "Purple Cow." People notice a "Purple Cow." Why? Because there aren't any. As I write this I am sitting at a Starbucks in Greenville, South Carolina. I have about an hour before my next meeting and I needed to find a place to grab a cup of "go juice" and crank out some writing. I passed several other establishments on my quest to find a Starbucks. I even made an illegal U-Turn to get here. Why? Because they are a "Purple Cow." I know that they have Wi-Fi so I can check and return emails, and I know that they won't mind me camping out for an hour to do so. While their product is coffee, their value is comfort. I am comfortable here, as are millions of others who frequent their stores. What's interesting is that directly across from this store sits another coffee house that has a sign on the side of their building that says, "You are fifty feet from better coffee!" Guess how many cars are in their lot? You guessed it...zero. The lack of customers in their store is not an indictment on the quality of their coffee. More accurately, it just shows how powerful the Starbucks brand has become.

Here is my question to you:

## WOULD YOUR CUSTOMERS DRIVE OUT OF THEIR WAY AND RISK A U-TURN TO DO BUSINESS WITH YOU?

# Chapter 8

# Teamwork Makes the Dream Work

"Even the Lone Ranger had Tonto."

- Jason Peacock

When was the last time you asked for help? More importantly, who did you ask? If you are struggling to come up with answers to the questions I have asked throughout this book, it could be because you are trying to answer them all by yourself. Why not enlist the help of others? This is another area where I think the school system has it all wrong. We force kids to go it alone when it comes to academia, and then can't figure out why they have trouble working with others. I was (and still am) a terrible test taker. What started as multiple choice quickly became multiple guess! If my teachers had only allowed me to partner up on tests, there is no telling how well I would have done in school. But no...they call that cheating. So instead of collaborating with others, I had to face the music alone and hope for a generous bell curve. If any of the above rings true for you, I have some great news: School's out!

Success in sales (and in life for that matter) is a team sport. Your ability to work with others toward a common objective is critical to winning. The late great speaker Jim Rohn put it this way: "It's hard to find a rich hermit." Far too often the sales profession is portrayed as "us versus them." The classic sales scene is two people sitting across the table from each other trading verbal jabs in a sort of non-contact jousting match. I don't know about you, but my knowledge of jousting is fairly limited. My only experience with the sport came as a result of my inability to choose a good destination for a date. As I mentioned earlier, the first date I took my wife on was to an art museum. To show my vast cultural appetite, I followed up the art museum visit with a date to a jousting competition. We went to a place called "Medieval Times." It was a large arena where you watch jousters compete, all while dining on such delicacies as Cornish Game Hen. The food was nothing to write home about, but the jousting was pretty cool. One thing is for certain: At the end of a match, there is one winner and one loser. There is no "win-win" in the sport of jousting. That is not the case in the game of selling. If you win and they lose, it won't be long before you will lose their business. If they win and you lose, you will regret the day you ever called on their account.

To create long term, mutually beneficial relationships, we have to "team up" with our customers. If your customers view you as simply a vendor, you will not keep their business for very long. However, if you are valuable part of their team, you are positioned for a long term relationship. One thing I have strived to do for my customers is to help them in areas other than just insurance. I clearly remember one of my clients thanking me for introducing them to my CPA. While I have served their insurance needs for several years, what they really benefited from was the service my CPA offered. Far too often we focus solely on our products and services instead of what our customers might really need. The next meeting you have with a client, instead of just talking about your services why not ask them what their most pressing business need is? What is keeping them up at night? If you can help them with that issue, your position on their team is that much more secure.

Teamwork not only helps in servicing existing customers, it can tremendously increase your odds of landing new business. I can tell you from personal experience that my closing ratio is much higher when I team up with a partner than when I fly solo. One advantage is that in a team setting, you have more than one set of eyes looking at the situation. While you are presenting to the potential client, your partner can watch for buying signals. After the meeting the team can discuss how the meeting really went and create a strategy for winning. It's similar to having a coach in the press box. The next time you watch a football game, look at the coaches on the sideline. Without exception they will all be wearing one thing in common. Any guesses as to what that is? The one thing all sideline coaches wear is a headset. Why? So they can communicate with the coaches in the press box. A coach that is at field level can't see what's really going on. Their view is blocked by the players. What they think is happening and what is really happening are often two different things. He thinks that the quarterback is not getting rid of the ball quick enough. The real problem is that the effort of the left tackle resembles that of a matador instead of a blocker. From the press box, the coaches are able to look down on the situation from a better vantage point. Their vision isn't blurred by being too close to the action. They can present an accurate picture to the field coaches who can make necessary adjustments. The same is true with Team Selling.

How about your team at the office? Do you view your associates as the "hired help" or as valued team members? My account executive Tricia Hushmire is my teammate. We win together, we lose together. Tricia has been my right and left hand for the past nine years. Many of my customers view her as their agent. Some guys would get a bruised ego from that...not me. The stronger her relationships are with my clients, the better we are able to serve them and the less likely they are to move their business.

Another key aspect of teamwork is our willingness to share the credit when things go well and take the blame when they fall apart. Those that are quick to take credit for their team's wins will never have sustained success. You can tell a lot about a person by how often they use the term, "I." If you find yourself "I"-ing in a presentation, substitute it with "we." "We" indicates that it's not all about you. I am sure you have heard the acronym for "TEAM." It is simply: Together Everyone Achieves More.

For teamwork to exist there must be a foundation of trust. Do you trust your team? What do you trust them with? Do you trust them to just process paperwork, or do you have full confidence that they "have your back." Try this next exercise sometime to truly understand trust: Go to any gas station in America and ask the local grease monkey for directions to the nearest mall. Here is what will happen: He will bend over backwards to give you those directions and will probably even draw you a map. Now, ask him for directions to his house. What?!? His smile is now gone and he is probably giving you what we in Georgia call the "Ol' Stink Eye!" So why was the same guy willing to give you a map to the mall but is unwilling to direct you to his home? Because the value has changed. When the value is small (the mall), trusting is easy; conversely when the value is high (his house, wife, kids, dog, truck on blocks), trusting is harder. Grease Monkey Joe has nothing to lose by giving you directions to the mall; therefore he is more than willing to help. Directions to his house given to the wrong person could be devastating, hence the reluctance. The same is true of our relationships.

If you find yourself checking up on their work "just to make sure" it has been done correctly, more than likely you have a trust issue. I have never understood people who hire others to assist them in their efforts, and then can't trust them to do quality work. Why did they hire them in the first place? The sooner you are able to trust your team, the sooner you will be able to practice the next principle we will discuss.

# Chapter 9

# One Trick Pony

*"Only do what only you can do."*

                    - Andy Stanley

As the New Guy, the thought of delegating tasks to others is a foreign concept. Right now you are responsible for every aspect of your business. There isn't enough business coming in yet to justify paying someone else to do the things you don't want to do. Another issue is some managers mistakenly believe that in order to learn the business, you need to spend time doing every aspect of it. Not true. You are paid to bring in business...period. You were not hired to be a receptionist, file clerk, janitor, or anything else for that matter. I am not demeaning any of those positions, they are all very important to an organization, but they are not your job. Like we discussed in Chapter seven, you have a unique set of skills and talents that you bring to the marketplace.

The marketplace demands excellence. It does not pay top dollar for average. I think a big reason that many people quit the sales profession is because they spend too much time trying to improve in areas where they will never be any good. Let me explain. I have never and will never be handy. I suffered a "mechanical bypass" as a child and have never recovered. My wife even went so far as to take away my one and only tool....my hammer. After an unsuccessful attempt to dislodge a pocket door, Wendy finally came to grips with the fact that her husband would forever be worthless as a fix-it man. I could spend the next several years attending every workshop that The Home Depot offers, and I would still be all thumbs. John Maxwell puts it this way: "Play to your strengths and delegate your weaknesses." If you are naturally good at something, why not pour on the effort to become great at it? Conversely, if you are naturally weak at something, why spend your precious time hoping to become mediocre? If you're not careful, you will find yourself spending a majority of your time shoring up your weaknesses instead of investing in your strengths. Go back to the quote at the beginning of this chapter. Read it a couple of times. The most successful people in any field live that statement. They know that time is fleeting, so if they are to maximize their personal production, they have to spend their time in their most effective areas... their "sweet spot." The classic book The Effective Executive by Peter Drucker addresses this issue: "Effective executives build on strengths... their own strengths....they do not build on weakness."

Think about your typical workday. What do you most enjoy? More than likely, it's what comes easy to you. We typically don't like difficult tasks. Think about this: what is it about the difficult task that makes it difficult? It's not the task itself, tasks are neutral. They are neither easy nor difficult. It is your ability to do them that makes them either easy or difficult. If you find yourself spending countless hours working hard, you are probably focusing on the wrong things. Now, I am not saying that you won't work some long hours, it just shouldn't be hard. Have you ever watched someone do something that on the surface looks difficult and said: "He makes it look so easy." Guess what? It is easy...for him. More than likely that person is very good at what he is doing and the reason is because he does it all the time. The reason they do it all the time? You guessed it: it's easy for him and he enjoys it; otherwise he wouldn't do it. Simple...isn't it?

When was the last time you went to a concert? If it's been awhile, I encourage you to go and check one out. Recently I had the privilege of taking my girls to see pop sensation Justin Bieber. My head is still ringing from the screaming of twenty thousand pre-teen girls. It was an experience I will never forget. All Bieber had to do was stand there and smile, and the girls went crazy! I have to admit, I was jealous. I have always wanted to be in a boy band but for whatever reason it hasn't happened...yet! Everyone in the arena knew beforehand he could sing, dance, and flip his "mop top" around with the best of them. What they didn't know until that moment is that he can play virtually any instrument. Throughout the show he would play some guitar, some piano, and even some drums. The important part of the last sentence is the word "some." Twenty thousand girls did not come to watch him tinker around with instruments...they came to listen and watch him croon. Justin Bieber gets paid ridiculous amounts of money to do what he does best...and he smiles the whole time he does it.

I read a quote several years ago about this principle. If you put it into practice it will change your life:

> The master in the art of living makes little distinction between his work and his play; his labor and his leisure; his mind and his body; his information and his recreation; his life and his religion. He hardly knows which is which. He simply pursues his vision of excellence at whatever he does, leaving others to decide whether he is working or playing. To him, he's always doing both.
>
> - James Michener

My challenge to you is this: If you haven't found your "sweet spot," find it. If you have, stay there. Don't apologize for being gifted in certain areas...play to your strengths! Working hard on your weaknesses only results in reinforcing them. Why do it?

# Chapter 10

# Tick-Tock

"Time is on my side."

- Mick Jagger

31,536,000. Care to guess what that number represents? That is the number of seconds that make up a year. Big number, isn't it? How about 525,600? That's the number of minutes in a year. So when a coworker asks you, "Do you have a minute?" of course you do...actually you have over half a million of them! What about something that takes an hour? You are still okay....you have 8,760 of them to spare. Only problem is that all of the above numbers are based on 365 days a year. Surely you don't work all of those do you? If you do, you need to put this book down and start working on your resume! Let's say you work forty hours a week for fifty weeks a year. You are now down to 2,000 hours. Now, think of all the hours you spend answering emails, attending worthless meetings, and eating lunch. Can you see how those 2,000 hours can get used up doing things that take you further away from your goals?

For the last thirteen plus years, I have worked with successful business owners in various industries. While their products and services may vary, there is one thing they all have in common. Without exception, they all value their time. At some point in their career they came to grips with the fact that Every Second Counts! Every moment of the day, you are either moving closer to, or further away from your goals. Out of everything we have discussed thus far, none is more important than how you handle your time. As the New Guy, you don't have the luxury of taking an extra half hour at lunch. That half hour becomes two and a half hours over the course of a week, and ten hours in a month. Ten hours! What could you have done with those ten hours? The sad thing is, you will never know.

The cruel thing about time is that once it's gone...it's gone. You can't "DVR" time. You can't pause or rewind a day. It's here and then it's gone...forever. Coach John Wooden had a statement that he preached to his players. It was simply, "Make every day a masterpiece." He would inform his players that if they only gave fifty percent effort today, they can't make it up by giving a hundred and fifty percent tomorrow. One hundred percent is all there is. You can't store up time to use at a later date. I don't want to get too philosophical, but have you ever stopped to think that there really is no such thing as "tomorrow"? When you get to tomorrow it's really today. Ok...that went a little too deep. What I am trying to say is that all we have to work with is this present moment.

We tend to think about time along the lines of a work week calendar. We work eight to five Monday through Friday. Friday evening comes and we get into weekend mode. Our mind goes into an "off" position for the next two days only to be jarred back into action Monday morning. Statistics show that there are more heart attacks on Monday mornings between the hours of four a.m. and ten a.m. than any other time of the week. Why is this? I think it's because we have conditioned ourselves to be "on" from eight to five and "off" once it's quitting time. When the alarm sounds Monday morning, we are reminded that it's back to work time and unfortunately for some people it's more than they can handle.

I will let you in on a little secret. If you are in sales or in business for yourself, you are always "on." I am not saying that you should be working 24/7, but you should always have your antennae up to catch ideas and thoughts that can help you. You never know where your next deal will come from. Several years ago I was at a local establishment watching an Elvis impersonator. Now before you laugh at me, understand that in Gainesville, Georgia, our options for nightlife are fairly limited. Somewhere in between "Heartbreak Hotel" and "Hound Dog," I happened to meet another Elvis fan who owned a company that was doing business with one of my clients. We traded business cards and since then he has become a referral source for me. As I said, you never know where your next deal will come from.

One of the biggest challenges you will face as The New Guy is determining what information is important and what isn't. As you get started, you will spend a mountain of time reading and re-reading emails that have zero impact on you and your career. Part of the reason you will do that is because we are made to feel guilty if we don't respond to or at least read everything that hits our inbox. You will often hear from coworkers, "Did you read my email?" You will politely say yes and maybe offer some commentary on it, all the while knowing that not only will you not go to their upcoming yard sale, you actually couldn't care less! I recently read a book that has completely changed my work life. It is titled, The 4-Hour Work Week, written by Timothy Ferris. As a result of applying the principles in the book, I currently have zero emails in my inbox. How many do you have? My desk has nothing on it other than my phone and computer. No files, no post it notes, nothing. For years, my inbox was packed full of half read emails that for the most part were absolutely worthless. The most important button on your computer is the delete button. The next time an email pops up on your screen, look at the subject line. That should tell you immediately if it's worth keeping or not. Odds are it isn't.

This type of thinking is counterintuitive. Most New Guys reason that since they have more time, they can take more time. Not true. The big producer in the next office actually has more time to "waste" than you do. He is already making the money you hope to make. He has a support staff that can handle a lot of the grunt work that you have to do yourself. You need to remember that to get where he is you have to do what he did. He can take off Friday's to play golf...you can't...yet.

# Chapter 11

# Person-ality

"I'm starting with the man in the mirror."

- Michael Jackson

Throughout the previous ten chapters, we have discussed the purpose, process, and principles of sales. In closing, I want to talk about the most important part of selling: the person.

A story is told of a young boy who was trying to get his dad to play with him while the dad was reading the newspaper. To buy himself some time, the dad took a page of the paper that had a picture of the world on it, tore it into pieces, and told his boy, "When you are done putting this picture back together we can play." To his astonishment the boy was back in just a couple of minutes with the world put back together. The boy explained to his surprised father that "On the other side of the paper there was a picture of a man. All I had to do was put him back together and the world just fell into place."

How is your world? How is your health? Are you working as hard on your cardio as you do on your quota? How about your spiritual life? When was the last time you went to church? How are your finances? I know, I know...you are the New Guy and aren't making any money yet. Well, how are you doing with what you are making?

How about stress? How are you holding up? Life will present you with tests, many of which are pop quizzes, which you are either prepared for or not. A few years ago I was popped with one that I failed miserably. We were headed to the airport to catch a flight for my brother's wedding. It was rush hour in Atlanta, which, if you haven't experienced it, just watch the next NASCAR race and you will know what it's like. As I attempted to change lanes, I stomped on the gas and quickly realized something was amiss. The pedal went to the floor but somehow I was slowing down! The transmission was going out, and what a perfect time to do so! I immediately turned off the radio (somehow I thought that would help matters), only to be greeted with the sound of a straining engine. We were now traveling at a top speed of approximately thirty mph, which was probably a good thing because we could barely decipher the expletives being hurled our way by the passing traffic. I was now sweating like Shaq at the foul line! I missed our exit to the parking lot because I could not get up enough speed to cross over the three lanes of traffic. Remember the scene from European Vacation when Clark Griswold "couldn't get left"? Only I didn't handle it quite so well. As we circled the airport for the fifth time, I began to punch the steering wheel like an angry Mike Tyson! I continued to reign down blows until something blew...the horn. Yep, the horn got stuck and I couldn't get it to stop blowing! So there we were, circling the airport, trying to exit, blinker on, horn blowing, kids crying, and blood pressure rising. Good times. We finally made it to the parking lot. We jumped out of the van, grabbed the luggage, and started our sprint to the terminal. When we reached the ticket counter, my son Tanner whispered to his mom, "Dad doesn't handle pressure very well, does he?" As my kids say, they had just witnessed an epic failure.

Get out your highlighter for this next statement. It comes from one of my favorite speakers, Jim Rohn. It is simply:

*"EVERYTHING AFFECTS*
*EVERYTHING ELSE."*

If you let your health slide you will probably be lax in your finances. The opposite is true as well. Whatever you improve helps you improve in other areas.

As your fitness improves, you will find that you have more energy at work. If you have more energy at work, your performance improves. Improved performance means you will make more money, and more money typically helps your stress level, which in turn helps your relationships. And to think, it all started with your fitness.

Another one of my favorite Rohn quotes is: "Wherever you are...be there." That one takes some thinking about. He is saying that wherever you currently are, be there. While you may wish to be somewhere else physically, financially, or relationally, don't miss the experience of where you are by wanting to be somewhere else.

From 1993–1995, I experienced one of the highest highs of my life and some of the lowest lows. The high was marrying Wendy. Everything else for the next two years was a low. It started going downhill when I was informed that the company I was working for no longer needed my service. They called it a downsizing, which is a pretty way of saying "you're fired." I was under-qualified to have the job in the first place, and I guess it finally caught up to me. So, armed with a handful of community college credits, I began the quest to find a career. What I found instead was a string of low paying dead end jobs. The first was as an assistant custodial engineer for a grocery store. My duties involved cleaning bathrooms, scrubbing floors, emptying grease traps, and shoveling snow. I know that sounds like a janitor, but my boss said I wasn't qualified for that title. I quickly moved up the ranks to become the "snow plow man." I would show up at the store at around four a.m., jump in the plow truck, and push snow until about noon. You may be thinking, "Eight hours of pushing snow?"

Let me explain. At the time, we were living at the northernmost part of Upper Michigan. It snows an average of 300 inches a year; hence the need for a full time plow boy. It was during the mindless hours of plowing that I was introduced to the world of personal development. I listened to every self improvement tape I could get my hands on. Hour after hour, guys like Jim Rohn, Zig Ziglar, and John Maxwell spoke into my life and gave me what I needed most...hope. I could have just as easily filled my head with Top 40 or Talk Radio. If I had gone that route, you would not be reading this. I did what most don't do.

## *I MAXIMIZED MY MINIMUM.*

To my boss, I was a minimum skill, minimum wage employee. I knew better. I knew that someday I would be paid, not for moving snow, but for "moving" people. My vision was to someday use the skills, experiences, and gifts that I have been given to do for others what the voices on those tapes did for me. This book is a result of what started in the cab of a snowplow.

What's your story? You may find yourself "plowing" through things on a daily basis that wear on your last nerve. Stay the course. The challenges you face today are preparing you for victory tomorrow. My favorite character from the Bible is David. We get to see him rise from lowly shepherd boy to Israel's greatest King. What I love about David is how he maximized his minimum. Think about this: David is most famous for one thing...killing Goliath. The skill he used to accomplish that was developed while watching sheep. Can you imagine a job more boring than watching sheep? After all, what is it again that we encourage our kids to do when they are having trouble falling asleep? That's right...count sheep! So, if the very act of counting sheep puts you to sleep, imagine doing it all day every day! And you thought your job was boring! David could have done what the other shepherds did...nothing. What he did was use his time in the field to prepare him for bigger and better things. How do I know this? Well, what did he kill Goliath with? A slingshot. By the time he faced off against Goliath, he was already an expert with a sling. It only took him one shot. Some of you may say, "That's true, but he took five stones just to be sure." Nope. Goliath had four brothers...David was ready for all of them! Think of the countless hours that he had spent practicing his sling shot. Business guru Malcolm Gladwell asserts that it takes ten thousand hours of dedicated practice to become an expert at something. My guess is that David had put in his ten thousand hours of sling work prior to meeting Goliath. The result? It's 2011 and Israel still marches under the flag of the Star of David.

I recently heard a great quote about success. It said, "A man's success is measured by how his kids describe him to their friends." As the New Guy, you will be pulled in several directions and you will never have enough time to get it all done. As we discussed in the previous chapter, there are some things you shouldn't be doing at all. As your schedule fills up, make sure you are the one filling it.

## YOU WILL HAVE TO LEARN TO SAY "NO" TO THE GOOD, SO THAT YOU CAN SAY "YES" TO THE BEST.

Are you more concerned about how your customers and coworkers feel about you than your family? You may say, "I love my family and after all, it's all about Quality Time, not Quantity." I read a book a few years ago that I highly recommend: Choosing to Cheat by Andy Stanley. The basic premise of the book is that you will cheat something: either your family or the marketplace. You have to choose which one. If you have to choose between missing a sale or a ball game... miss the sale. Money will come again, childhood doesn't. On the walls of my office are pictures of the most important people in my life...my family. I don't have a single framed picture of an insurance policy. Making money is great...making memories is priceless!

Remember, there is only one place where you can't be replaced: Your home. This next statement will change your life...if you will let it. It is a quote by business strategist, Joey Reiman. He said: "The road to success just might be your driveway."

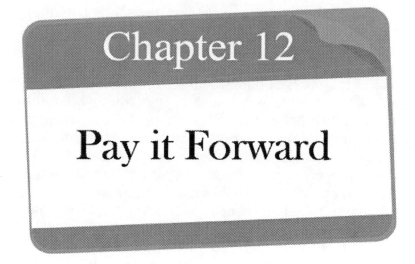

# Chapter 12

# Pay it Forward

*"You can have everything in life you want, if you will just help enough other people get what they want."*

- Zig Ziglar

I was eighteen years old selling newspapers door-to-door in the Chicago area. Everyone should have this experience at least once in their life. Our "boss" Alex (who was all of nineteen years old) would pile all of us peddlers into his Suburban, take us to a neighborhood, and drop us off. We would scatter throughout the streets and meet back at a prearranged time, hoping to have a pocket full of orders. One particular night, Alex chose an upscale neighborhood for us. My first thought was, "These rich people aren't going to buy my lousy newspaper...and they will probably be mad at me for interrupting their evening." I will never forget walking up to that first door. I knocked–softly–hoping they wouldn't come to the door. I was in the process of walking away when the door opened. Inside the doorway stood a guy who was dressed for success. I specifically remember his shoes; they looked like they had just been shined (if you are from Chicago you know how hard it is to keep your shoes shiny in the winter). Anyway, he stood there awaiting my pitch. With all the confidence of a recent Dale Carnegie graduate, I began my presentation. I believe it went something like this: "You don't want to buy a newspaper do you?" I wasn't ready for his answer. "No I don't. I want to buy *all* of them." Can you believe it?! One sales call and I was sold out! Even better, he invited me in from the cold and let me have dinner with his family! They (I should say "We") had steak! As I was leaving the nicest home I had ever been in, this man took an opportunity to "pay it forward." He smiled and told me that when he was a young man, he too earned his stripes as a door-to-door salesman. He will never know the impact that had on a young eighteen-year-old boy.

That's really what this book is about. I want to be that guy for you. As I mentioned in the introduction, this is a tough job. It will present you with challenges on a daily basis. There will be days when you would rather skin dive for Roto Rooter. Trust me...it gets easier. I have a picture in my office that I look at often. It is of John Akhwari of Tanzania. He competed in the 1968 Olympics in Mexico City as a marathon runner. He didn't win a medal. What he did win was the admiration and respect of all who heard his story. During the race, John fell and severely injured his leg. Instead of quitting, he hobbled the 26.2 miles and finished...in last place. When the T.V. reporters interviewed him he simply said, "My country didn't send me 5,000 miles to start the race. They sent me 5,000 miles to finish."

There have been many days when I have felt like John Akhwari. How about you? John taped up and ran. He played while hurt. He finished. You can too.

My own personal "Olympics" moment happened in 1986. I was an undersized eighth grader with all the confidence of a mathlete. For the past two years I had endured a very difficult middle school experience. In the seventh grade my family moved cross country from a very small town in Louisiana to the big city of Chicago. You might say it was culture shock. In the spring of 1985, I chose not to compete at Field Day. While the other kids ran races, I stood on the sidelines watching. I knew I was faster than any of them, but was paralyzed by the fear of ridicule if I didn't win. For the seventh straight year, the sprint champion blew away the competition...*her* name was Kim Bombacino. Fast forward to eighth grade. The sign up list for Field Day was posted on our class room wall. Directly below

"Fifty-yard dash" was a single name...Kim. No last name needed. For the previous seven years, she had become a legend by beating everybody. Boy, girl, didn't matter. With a trembling hand I scrawled my name below hers...Jason Peacock. In a matter of minutes, the news spread throughout the school that I was going to challenge Kim for the coveted title of "fastest kid in the school." With two weeks to prepare, I embarked upon a strict training regimen that Rocky himself would be proud of...the only thing missing was a chicken to chase. Every day at school, the pressure mounted. I would be lying if I didn't tell you that I too had doubts. She was fast, and more daunting was the fact that she was a girl! Can you imagine losing to a girl in middle school? My life would be over if she beat me. Something like that has afterschool special written all over it! As D-Day approached, my dad stepped in, kinda like Rocky's trainer, Mickey. He reminded me of my own past successes. You see, I too was undefeated. I had never lost a race at Field Day, and he reasoned that if I could win at my old school, there was no reason I couldn't win at my new one. Race day came and I was amped up like a thoroughbred at the Derby. Time for one last pep talk. Pops pulled me aside and said, "After you win, be a gentleman. She will be very upset and embarrassed, so be extra kind to her."

After I win?!? He had no doubt. A few seconds later, neither did anyone else. That win was monumental for me. Yes, I know it was only the eighth grade and I was racing a girl. A girl, by the way, that went on to break stolen base records in softball for the State of Illinois. But it was more than that. It showed me who was in my corner: My family. No one else thought I would win. I did and my family did, and that is all that mattered.

Have you ever watched a prize fight? Where does the trainer, the "Corner Man," stand in relation to the boxer? The answer: It depends on how the boxer is doing. If his fighter is getting beat, the trainer will stand directly in front of him shielding him from seeing the guy who is beating him. He will remind him of the training they have done, how he has what it takes to win, how he has the "Eye of the Tiger." If the boxer is winning, he will stand behind him rubbing his shoulders, speaking into the ear of his warrior telling him, "Look across the ring at him. Look at how you are beating him. Now finish him off!"

My goal for this book is to accomplish one thing: To be your "Corner Man." To give you Hope. If a guy with nothing more than a high school degree, and a handful of community college credits can move into a town where he doesn't know a soul and build a successful business, then you can too!

I will never forget when I witnessed firsthand the amazing power of hope. Wendy and I were at a video rental store getting our movie for the night when a young mother and her two little boys entered the store. As little boys will do, they entered like a bull in a china shop. They immediately saw the gumball machine and made a beeline for it. Inside the machine were various toys and trinkets, but one in particular toy had caught their eye. They ran to their mom and said, "Mom! Mom! That machine has a Detroit Red Wings yo-yo...give me some money so I can win it!" Their mom bristled at the request and snapped back, "Son, you won't win it! Life never works out like you want it to. The sooner you learn that, the better!" The words came from a voice of experience. From the looks of things, her life had not worked out like she had planned. Two kids...one parent...no ring...no hope. I wasn't about to stand there and let her steal their hope. I grabbed Wendy's purse and headed for the gumball machine. I motioned for the boys to join me in our quest for the yo-yo. Quarter by quarter our excitement increased as we got closer to the elusive yo-yo. Finally, our persistence paid off. As the yo-yo fell, three hearts soared...two little boys and a man with quarters.

## LIFE IS LIKE THAT GUMBALL MACHINE. WE STAND LOOKING INTO IT AND HOPE WE HAVE ENOUGH QUARTERS.

I have good news for you. There is someone who never runs out. One of my favorite Bible verses is Jeremiah 29:11. God says, "For I know the plans I have for you. Plans to prosper you, not to harm you. Plans to give you hope and a future."

Now that you are done with this book, all I ask is that, when the time is right, please pass it along to The New Guy.

God Bless,
Jason